WunderKeys Piano For Preschoolers
Book 1 - Sorting Sounds

Andrea Dow and Trevor Dow

Visit **www.WunderKeys.com** for teacher's manual and supplementary lesson materials.

Copyright © 2011 Teach Music Today Learning Solutions
2152 Wildflower Dr., Shawnigan Lake, BC, V0R 2W1

All Rights Reserved. Printed in U.S.A.

The music, text, design, and graphics in this publication are protected by copyright law. Any duplication is an infringement of copyright law.

"Hello! My name is **Maestro Matthew**. I love to play the piano. I also love to learn math. Guess what? We can do both… at the same time!"

Lesson 1 - Meet the Finger Friends

Can you stick out your thumbs? Your thumbs are called **Thumbelina**. Can you make Thumbelina dance? Play any key on the piano with Thumbelina.

Point at the piano. These fingers are called **Pointer Panda.** Can you make Pointer Panda wiggle? Play any key on the piano with Pointer.

Middleton Mouse lives in the middle of your hand. Can you make him dance? Play any key on the piano with Middleton.

Ringo Raccoon is very shy. He lives next to Middleton Mouse. He doesn't like to stand up on his own. Can you make Ringo do a shy dance? Play any key on the piano with Ringo.

Pinky Pig is just a baby. He is the smallest finger. Can you make Pinky wiggle? Play any key on the piano with Pinky.

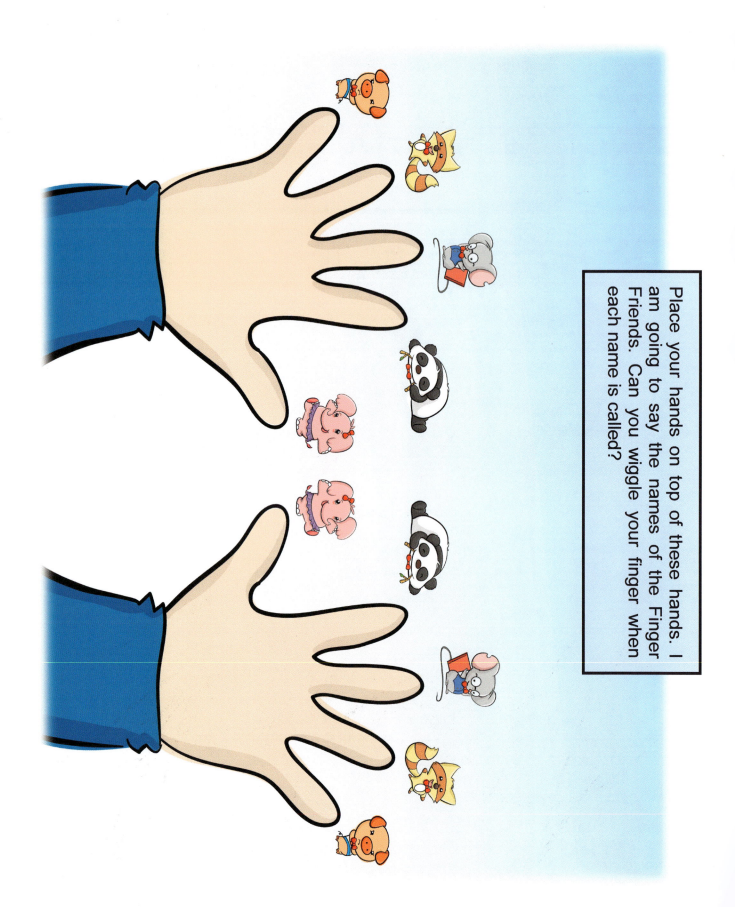

Place your hands on top of these hands. I am going to say the names of the Finger Friends. Can you wiggle your finger when each name is called?

Lesson 1 - Home Activity
My Finger Friends

Activity #1

In your lesson you learned the names of your Finger Friends. Can you complete the activity below with your mom or dad?

Circle Thumbelina and then point to your Thumbelina Finger.

Circle Middleton Mouse and then point to your Middleton Finger.

Circle Pointer Panda and then point to your Pointer Finger.

Circle Ringo Raccoon and then point to your Ringo Finger.

Circle Pinky Pig and then Point to your Pinky Finger.

Activity #2

1. Review the sheets that you learned in your lesson.

2. Practice playing sounds on the piano with each of your Finger Friends. Can you play a sound with your Thumbelina? Can you play a sound with your Pointer Panda?

3. Have your mom or dad point to each of your fingers. Can you tell your mom or dad each finger's name?

Dancing is a great way for your Finger Friends to warm up before they play the piano. Make them dance every day before you practice.

Lesson 2 - Dancing with my Finger Friends

The Finger Friends love to dance! I am going to point to a Finger Friend. Can you make that friend wiggle and dance?

Look at the three pictures of the Finger Friends below. Maestro Matthew has put a circle around groups of Finger Friends who are the same and an "X" through groups of Finger Friends who are different.

Now try it on your own!

Look at the three pictures of the Finger Friends below. If a picture shows three Finger Friends who are the same, circle it. If a picture shows three Finger Friends who are different, put an "X" through it.

Playing the Piano with my Finger Friends

"It's pretty fun playing the piano. I think I'm really going to like learning how," said Middleton Mouse, twitching his tail excitedly. "What is the first thing we get to learn?"

"Well," said Ringo, "I think we need to know when to play a sound!"

"That's easy!" giggled Middleton Mouse. "When we see our picture on our music page, it means we should play a sound with that Finger Friend!"

"That *is* easy!" said Ringo. "I see all of our pictures down there. Which one should I play first?"

When I point to a picture of a Finger Friend, play any key on the piano using that finger.

Lesson 2 - Home Activity
Same and Different

Activity #1

Put an "X" through the boxes that have Finger Friends who are different. Put a circle around the boxes that have Finger Friends who are the same.

Activity #2

1. Review the sheets that you learned in your lesson.

2. Practice playing sounds on the piano with each of your Finger Friends. Can you play a key with your Pinky Pig? Can you play a key with your Thumbelina? Try them all.

3. The piano has black and white keys. Use your Thumbelina to play all of the black keys. Use your Pointer Panda to play all of the white keys.

When you hold a little kitten you have to be very gentle. How would you hold a little kitten in the palm of your hand? Can you show me?

Great! That's how your fingers should curve when you play the piano.

Lesson 3 - Playing the Piano with Polite Fingers

"Pianos are fun because they can make a lot of noise!" said Thumbelina as she stomped on the keys as loudly as she could. The other Finger Friends just watched her play.

"What's the matter? Come join me!" said Thumbelina.

"We think it sounds nicer when you play without stomping," Ringo said quietly. "It sounds more like music."

The other Finger Friends nodded. "Yes it sounds much better," they said.

Can you try playing "thumpy" like Thumbelina? Now try playing carefully like Ringo. Which sounds more like music?

Try This!

Close your eyes. I will play sounds that are "polite" and sounds that are "rude." Hold up your Thumbelina if you a hear a rude sound, and hold up your Ringo Raccoon if you hear a polite sound.

Now let's switch roles. You play the sounds and I will hold up my fingers.

High Sounds and Low Sounds

"Dancing sure is fun," said Thumbelina to Pinky Pig. "Look at all those keys on the piano! Listen to all the beautiful sounds they make." She began to dance on the low keys.

Pinky Pig snorted, "You're giving me a headache. There must be better sounds for a little pig like me."

Finding High Sounds and Low Sounds

Where do you think the high piggy sounds are on the piano? Can you point to them on your piano?

Where do you think the low elephant sounds are on the piano? Can you point to them on your piano?

Activity #1

We're going to play a game. Close your eyes and listen to the music. If I am playing a low elephant sound, hold up your Thumbelina. If I am playing a high piggy sound, hold up your Pinky Pig.

Activity #2

Watch my hands. If I hold up my Thumbelina, play a low elephant sound. If I hold up my Pinky Pig, play a high piggy sound.

Lesson 3 - Home Activity
Piano Manners

Activity #1

In your lesson, you learned how to play the piano with polite fingers. Thumbelina was playing rude sounds, and Ringo Raccoon was playing polite sounds. Look at the pictures below. When your mom or dad points to Thumbelina, play a rude sound. When your mom or dad points to Ringo, play a polite sound.

Activity #2

Now your parent will play high and low sounds. If you hear a high sound, circle Pinky Pig. If you hear a low sound, circle Thumbelina.

1.   2.   3.

Activity #3

1. Review the sheets that you learned in your lesson.

2. Practice playing rude sounds and polite sounds.

3. When we sit at the piano, we try to sit with a straight back and nicely curved fingers, with our legs hanging down off the piano bench. Can you show your parent how you are supposed to sit at the piano? Now can you show how not to sit at the piano?

Can you play any key with your Middleton Mouse?

I will show you how Middleton can play a high sound and a low sound on the piano. Can you do this all by yourself?

Lesson 4 - Middleton Mouse Climbs a Ladder

1.

2.

Middleton Mouse rested his paws on a ladder. "I like to climb up ladders because I can climb way up high or climb way down low. I'm so little, I have to use one to reach the piano keys!"

"Let's play! If you see me up high on the ladder, play a high sound. If you see me down low on the ladder, play a low sound. Try numbers 1 through 4 on this page twice. Then try them out of order!"

3.

4.

Can you show high and low?

Try This!

Close your eyes and listen to the sounds I am going to play.

Is Middleton Mouse playing high sounds or low sounds?

Get a marker ready. If I play a high sound, put a dot up high on a ladder. If I play a low sound, put a dot down low on a ladder.

Middleton Mouse was having a great time! He climbed up and down the ladders, careful to keep his tail from getting tangled in the rungs. "Can we do more?" he panted as he ran up and down. "I just love to hear high and low sounds."

Pointer Panda watched him sleepily "Aren't you getting tired? Come and take a nap with me."

"Nope!" Middleton did a dance at the bottom of one ladder. "I've got lots of energy. Let's keep going! It sounds like music!"

Lesson 4 - Home Activity
High Sounds and Low Sounds

Activity #1

In your lesson, you learned that there are high sounds and low sounds on the piano. Your parent will point to any picture below. If you see Middleton up high on the ladder, use your Middleton Mouse to play a high sound. If you see Middleton down low on the ladder, use your Middleton Mouse to play a low sound.

1.
2.
3.
4.
5.
6.

Activity #2

Do the same activity again, but this time play the pictures in order starting at "1". Can you play the sounds while saying "high" or "low"?

Activity #3

1. Review the sheets that you learned in your lesson.

2. Practice playing high and low sounds with each of your Finger Friends.

3. Make up your own song on the piano using high and low sounds, and play it for your mom or dad. Write the name of your piece below.

"Look!" Thumbelina nudged Ringo. "Pointer Panda is on the ladder now." They giggled as they watched him try to climb with bamboo in his hand.

He slowly made his way up the ladder, pausing sometimes to take a break in the middle.

"Could someone help?!" he called out.

Lesson 5 - Climb the Ladder Cut-out

Try This!

Use your Pointer Panda to play the high or low sounds for the pictures below. What do you think you should play if Pointer is in the middle of the ladder?

Let's cut out the pictures below one row at a time and paste them onto the "Climb the Ladder" page. Put the pictures in order showing Pointer Panda moving from low to high on the ladder.

Row #1

Row #2

Row #3

Climb the Ladder

Collect the pictures of Pointer Panda that you cut out from the previous page.

Can you paste the pictures from each row in order? Pointer Panda starts low on the ladder and climbs higher.

Once you have the pictures in order, play the sounds on the piano. There are low sounds, middle sounds, and high sounds.

Row 1

Row 2

Row 3

Lesson 5 - Home Activity
Climb the Ladder

Activity #1

Look at the pictures below. If you see Pointer Panda up high on a ladder, play a high sound. If he is down low on a ladder, play a low sound. What should you do if he is in the middle of the ladder?

Activity #2

Your mom or dad will play seven sounds up high or down low. When you hear your mom or dad play a low sound, put a checkmark in the box beside the ladder that shows Pointer Panda sitting low. If you hear a high sound, put a checkmark in the box beside the ladder that shows Pointer Panda sitting high.

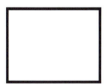   

Activity #3

1. Review the sheets that you learned in your lesson.

2. Can you use low sounds to make up a song about a thunderstorm? Can you use high sounds to make up a song about a baby bunny rabbit?

Lesson 6 - Long and Short Sounds

"Whew, I'm tired," said Pointer Panda. "All of that climbing makes me sleepy. My legs are so tired that I'm walking as slowly as Thumbelina."

Thumbelina grinned at him, "You try walking quickly when you're my size! Elephants take longer to move."

"I like being quick," said Ringo. He took several fast steps to show off how fast he could move. "I need to be quick to hide in the shadows at night."

Middleton Mouse was watching his friends and playing with his whiskers, deep in thought. "Hey, everyone . . . do you think we could play long, lazy sounds like Thumbelina and quick short sounds like Ringo on the piano?"

Try This!

We're going to play a game. Close your eyes and tell me whether I am playing a long, lazy elephant sound or a short, quick raccoon sound. If you hear a long sound, hold up your Thumbelina. If you hear a short sound, hold up your Ringo Raccoon.

Now it's your turn to play the piano. Watch my hands. If I hold up my Thumbelina, play a long sound. If I hold up my Ringo, play a short sound.

"I want to play long and short sounds!" Middleton was so excited that he accidentally tripped over his tail as he rushed toward the piano.

"Are you OK, Middleton?" Pinky Pig nudged his friend with his snout.

"I think so," Middleton said, inspecting his paws carefully. "I think I can still play."

"I'll come with you," Pinky Pig whispered to Middleton. "I haven't had a turn in a long time!"

Playing with long and short sounds

Try This!

Find your Pinky Pig and Middleton Mouse fingers. Can you make Middleton play a long sound? Can you make Pinky Pig play a short sound?

Look below to see if the pictures show short sounds or long sounds. Can you make your Finger Friend play what you see below on any key?

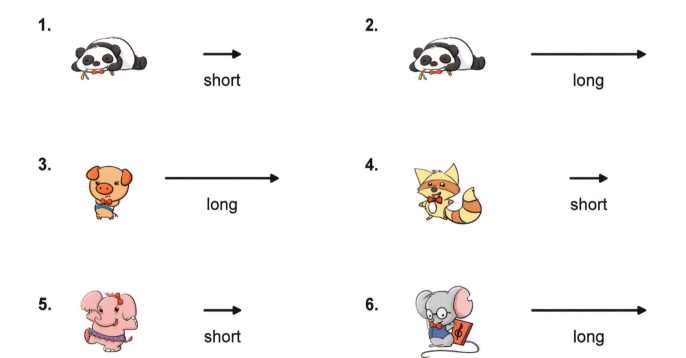

Lesson 6 - Home Activity
Long and Short Sounds

Activity #1

In your lesson, you learned that sounds played on the piano can be long or short. Beside the pictures of Pointer Panda, draw long or short lines, then play the sounds you have drawn.

Activity #2

Your mom or dad will play seven long sounds or short sounds. If you hear a long sound, put a checkmark next to the picture of Pointer Panda above a long sound. If you hear a short sound, put a checkmark next to the picture of Pointer Panda above a short sound.

 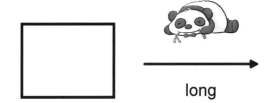

Activity #3

1. Review the sheets that you learned in your lesson.

2. Can you play short sounds on white keys? Can you play long sounds on black keys?

3. Have your mom or dad close their eyes. Play a long sound or a short sound. Have them tell you what they heard. Now it's your turn to close your eyes, and your mom or dad will play the long and short sounds. Can you guess what they played?

"How long can you hold a sound?" Thumbelina bunched up her trunk and held her breath. "Short . . . sounds . . . are . . . easier!" She struggled to keep the air in.

"You can breathe when you play a sound!" Ringo giggled as Thumbelina started to turn blue.

Lesson 7 - Practicing with Long and Short Sounds

Try This!

Let's cut out these pictures and paste them onto the "Play With Me" page. Put the sound pictures in order from shortest sound to longest sound for each set of Finger Friends pictures.

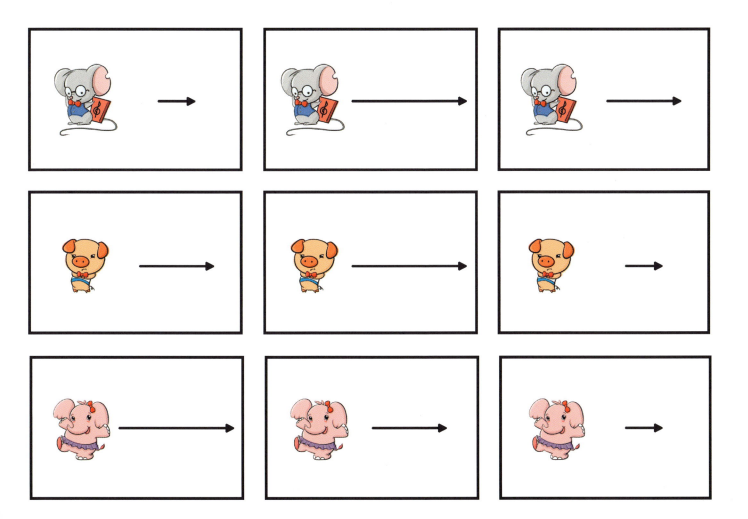

Play With Me!

Try This!

Have you cut out all the pictures? Can you put the pictures in order from shortest sounds to longest sounds? Put the same Finger Friend in each row.

Once you have the pictures in order, play the sounds on the piano. There are short sounds, medium sounds, and long sounds.

Middleton Mouse

Pinky Pig

Thumbelina

Lesson 7 - Home Activity
Practicing with Long and Short

Activity #1

Have your mom or dad help you cut out the pictures of Thumbelina playing short sounds and long sounds. Can you paste them in order from shortest to longest in the gray boxes below?

Try playing the sounds in order. Use your Thumbelina. Play the sounds on a high key. Play the sounds on a low key. Now try using a different Finger Friend.

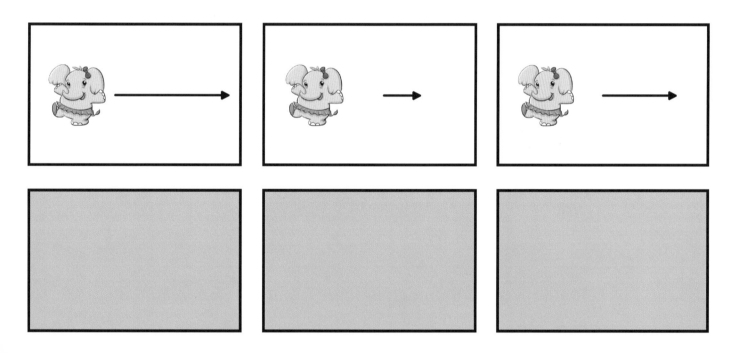

Activity #2

1. Review the sheets that you learned in your lesson.

2. Can you play short sounds on high keys? Can you play long sounds on low keys?

3. Make up a song about a lazy sloth that meets a quick rabbit. Can you imagine what would happen? Where should there be short and long sounds? Play your song for your mom or dad and explain what is happening.

As hard as they tried, the Finger Friends could not fit the piano into Middleton's house. The piano was just too big, and Middleton's house was just too small.

"Sometimes it's no fun being small," sobbed Middleton.

"Don't worry," said Pointer Panda. "Let's go get you a smaller piano."

Lesson 8 - Sorting Big and Small

Can you help Middleton and Thumbelina find their instruments?

Draw an "X" through the instruments that would fit in Middleton's small house.

Draw a circle around the instruments that Thumbelina would put in her big house.

Black Notes ... Big and Small

"Eww!" Middleton Mouse looked at Pinky Pig with distaste. "You're all covered in mud!"

"Mud makes me so happy!" Pinky snorted. "It keeps me cool when it's sunny outside."

But where did you find the mud puddles?" Middleton asked as he watched a glob of dirt drip from Pinky's nose.

"On the piano," Pinky replied. "I pretend that the black keys are mud puddles. They come in groups that are big and small . . . big mud puddles and small mud puddles."

"Can you show me which ones are the small mud puddles on the piano?" Middleton asked. He was interested. "Then I'll be able to find the big mud puddles too!"

"Sure, let's go!" said Pinky Pig.

Look at the black keys below.

Can you find the big group of black keys?

Can you find the small group of black keys?

Can you find all of these "mud puddles" on the piano?

Splashing in the Mud

Can you find the mud puddles on the piano? Use your Finger Friends to jump from one mud puddle to the next all the way up the piano. Make a loud "splat" sound! Make sure you look to see whether the mud puddle has room for two Finger Friends or three Finger Friends.

Lesson 8 - Home Activity
Sorting Big and Small

Activity #1

In your lesson, you learned how to sort big and small instruments. Can you circle the biggest instrument in red and the smallest instrument in blue?

1.

2.

Activity #2

Black keys on the piano come in big groups (big mud puddles) and small groups (small mud puddles). Can you circle the big mud puddles in red and the small mud puddles in blue?

Activity #3

1. Review the sheets that you learned in your lesson.

2. Practice playing high and low sounds with each of your Finger Friends.

3. Can you find all of the "big mud puddles" on the piano? Start low, and play all of them until you get to the highest sounds on the piano.

Congratulations! You have made it to the last lesson in Book 1. I hope you have enjoyed your journey. Let's take a look at everything you have learned!

Lesson 9 - Look What I Have Learned!

"I've learned so much about the piano!" Pinky Pig exclaimed as he curled and uncurled his tail in excitement. "I can't wait to tell my piggy friends all about high and low, big and small, long and short, black and white. "Let's play with everything we've learned, OK?"

"Yeah, let's see if we can do it all by ourselves!" the other Finger Friends yelled as they rushed to the piano.

"Maestro Matthew, you ask the questions and we'll answer!"

High and Low

If you see Pointer Panda high on a ladder, play a high black key. If you see Pointer Panda low on a ladder, play a low black key.

Long and Short

Thumbelina is tired. She can play only long sounds today. Ringo is excited. He is playing only short sounds today. Look at the pictures of each Finger Friend below. Play short sounds if the picture shows a short line, and play long sounds if the picture shows a long line. Are you using the correct Finger Friend to play each sound?

 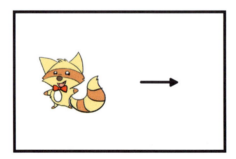 

All Together Now

Pointer and Middleton are playing long and short sounds up high and down low! Today, Pointer plays long sounds, and Middleton plays short sounds. Look at the pictures below. If Pointer is up high on the ladder, play a long sound on a high key using your Pointer Panda. If Pointer is low on the piano, play a long sound on a low key using your Pointer Panda. Do the same for Middleton Mouse, but use short sounds instead.

Congratulations!

Student Name

Teacher Name: _____   Date: _____

Certificate of Completion: Book 1

Printed in Great Britain
by Amazon.co.uk, Ltd.,
Marston Gate.